Pegan Diet Cookbook

for

Beginners

By

G. Noble

Pegan Diet Cookbook for Beginners

By

G. Noble

Published By: Unicorn Publishers

Copyright © 2021 G. Noble.

<u>Cover Design By:</u>

S. Pablo

<u>Content Source:</u>

sunkissedkitchen

merakilane

healthline

&

cookinglight

Table of Content

06. *Salad with Spinach and Bacon Dressing.*

07. *Roasted Beef Tenderloin*

08. *Sausage Spaghetti Squash Boats*

09. *Soup With Chicken, Zoodles, And Sweet Potatoes (Thai Red Curry)*

10. *Creamy Tuscan Garlic Chicken*

10 PEGAN Diet Recipe For Dinner:

01. *Salad Of Pan-Seared Salmon, Kale, And Apple*

02. *Slow Cooker Spicy Beef Curry Stew*

03. *Wraps Of Tempeh Lettuce With Peanut Sauce (Vegan)*

04. *Salad With The Ultimate Chicken Tacos*

05. *Sweet Potato Pizza Crust*

06. *Salad Of Thai Mangoes And Avocados With Grilled Sweet Potatoes*

07. *Roasted Vegetable & Lentil Salad With Coriander Yoghurt Dressing*

08. *Mexican Toasted Corn Quinoa Salad*

09. *Sweet Potatoes With Lemony Kale And White Beans*

10. *Baked Salmon With Black Rice*

The Gist

What Is The Pegan Diet All About?

The Pegan diet is a plant-based food pattern that incorporates elements of both the paleo and vegan diets. Although these two diets are mutually exclusive in certain respects (for example, the paleo diet allows for the consumption of eggs and beef, while the vegan diet prohibits the consumption of all animal products and byproducts), the focus is on consuming whole foods. By suppressing inflammation and regulating blood sugar, the pegan diet encourages good wellbeing. The pegan diet emphasizes vegetables, fruits, nuts, seeds, meat, fish, and eggs while excluding the majority of dairy, grains, legumes, beans, sugar, and refined foods.

What Are The Pegan Diet's Benefits?

The pegan diet places a premium on nutrient-dense fruits and vegetables, which means it has a plethora of health benefits. Fruits and vegetables are high in fibre, vitamins, minerals, and antioxidants, both of which contribute to disease prevention. Unsaturated fats from seafood, beans, and nuts may help improve heart wellbeing, and the pegan diet eating plan's focus on whole, unprocessed foods is certain to minimize inflammation.

Consumables

The Pegan diet places a premium on whole grains, or foods that have been processed minimally or not at all before reaching your plate.

Consume A Variety Of Plants

Vegetables and fruit are the main food groups for the pegan diet; they can account for 75% of your overall consumption.

To lower the blood sugar reaction, low-glycemic fruits and vegetables, such as berries and non-starchy vegetables, should be prioritized.

For those who have already maintained healthy blood sugar management prior to beginning the diet, small quantities of starchy vegetables and sugary fruits may be permitted.

Select Protein That Has Been Safely Sourced.

If the pegan diet focuses on plant-based diets, sufficient protein consumption from animal sources is also recommended.

Bear in mind that since 75% of the diet is composed of vegetables and meat, less than a quarter of the diet is composed of animal-based proteins. As a result, you'll consume far less meat than you will on a traditional paleo diet — but much more than you will on a vegan diet.

The pegan diet strictly prohibits the consumption of conventionally farmed meats and eggs. Other than that, it emphasizes grass-fed, pasture-raised cattle, pork, chickens, and whole eggs.

Additionally, it promotes the consumption of fish — especially those with a low mercury content, such as sardines and wild salmon.

Consume Fats That Have Been Minimally Refined.

On this diet, you can consume healthy fats from a variety of sources, including the following:
- Any nuts, except peanuts.
- Any seeds, except seed oils that have been refined.
- Olives and avocados: Additionally, cold-pressed olive and avocado oils can be used.
- Cocoa: Coconut oil that has not been distilled is allowed.
- Omega-3 fatty acids: Especially those derived from mercury-free fish or algae
- Additionally, grass-fed, pasture-raised meats and whole eggs contribute to the pegan diet's fat content.

Consumption of some whole grains and legumes is permitted.

While the majority of grains and legumes are prohibited on the pegan diet due to their ability to affect blood sugar, certain gluten-free whole grains and legumes are allowed in moderation.

Consumption of grains should not exceed 1/2 cup (125 grams) per meal, and legumes should not exceed 1 cup (75 grams) per day.

You will consume the following grains and legumes: Black rice, quinoa, amaranth, millet, teff, and oats, Lentils, chickpeas, black beans, and pinto beans. However, if you have diabetes or another disease that leads to low blood sugar regulation, you should limit these foods even more.

10 Pegan Diet Foods

01. Vegetables that are not starchy and plenty of leafy greens
02. Berries
03. A variety of nuts, such as almonds, pistachios, and walnuts
04. Flax, chia, and pumpkin seeds
05. Beef, ham, and pork raised on grass
06. Fish
07. Eggs
08. Avocado and olive oils
09. Lentils, chickpeas, black beans, and pinto beans are also legumes.
10. Cereal grains, such as black rice and quinoa.

Avoid These Foods

The pegan diet is more adaptable than the paleo or vegan diets due to its allowance of nearly any meal on an occasional basis.

Several diets and food types, however, are highly discouraged. Some ingredients are well-known to be harmful, while others are found very safe — depending on who you ask.

On A Pegan Diet, These Items Are Usually Avoided:

Dairy: It is highly prohibited to consume cow's milk, yoghurt, or cheese. Foods made from sheep or goat milk, on the other hand, are allowed in small amounts. Occasionally, grass-fed butter is permitted as well.

Gluten: All gluten-containing grains should be avoided at all costs.

Gluten-free foods: Even gluten-free grains are prohibited. Occasionally, small quantities of gluten-free whole grains can be allowed.

Legumes: The majority of legumes are avoided due to their ability to raise blood sugar levels. Legumes with a low starch content, such as lentils, may be allowed.

Sugar: Added sugar of any form, refined or unrefined, is generally avoided. It can be seen on occasion — but only with extreme caution.

Refined oils: Oils that have been refined or heavily processed, such as canola, soybean, sunflower, and corn oil, are almost always avoided.

Artificial colorings, flavours, and preservatives, as well as other contaminants, are avoided.

The majority of these ingredients are restricted due to their alleged effect on blood sugar and/or inflammation in the body.

09 Foods to Avoid on Pegan Diet

01. Dairies
02. Cereals
03. Glucosamine
04. Legumes
05. Beans
06. Sucrose
07. Foods that have been processed, such as pizza and French fries
08. Refined oils, such as those from canola, sunflower, rice, and soybean
09. Food additives such as chemical flavours and colours

Potential Advantages

The pegan diet can have a variety of beneficial effects on your health.

Perhaps its strongest feature is its heavy focus on fruit and vegetable consumption.

Fruits and vegetables are nutritious powerhouses. They're packed with fibre, vitamins, minerals, and phytochemicals that have been shown to avoid disease and minimize oxidative stress and inflammation.

Additionally, the pegan diet stresses the use of nutritious, unsaturated fats from fish, nuts, seeds, and other plants, which can have a beneficial effect on heart health.

Additionally, diets that are high in whole foods and low in ultra-processed foods are associated with an increase in the overall consistency of the diet.

Consequences

Despite its benefits, the pegan diet does have some drawbacks worth mentioning.

Restrictions That Are Not Required

While the pegan diet allows for more variety than either the vegan or paleo diets alone, many of the proposed restrictions exclude very nutritious foods such as legumes, whole grains, and dairy.

The pegan diet's proponents also cite heightened inflammation and blood sugar elevation as key factors for eliminating these foods.

Naturally, certain may have allergies to gluten and dairy products, which can trigger inflammation. Similarly, some individuals have difficulty controlling their blood sugar when they consume high-starch foods such as wheat or legumes.

Reduced or complete elimination of these foods can be necessary in these instances.

However, whether you have serious allergies or intolerances, avoiding them is superfluous.

Additionally, if large classes of foods are eliminated arbitrarily, nutritional shortages will result if such nutrients are not carefully substituted. As a result, you can need a clear understanding of nutrition in order to safely follow the pegan diet.

Inaccessibility

While a diet rich in organic fruits and vegetables and grass-fed, pasture-raised meats may sound ideal in principle, it may be out of reach for many people.

To be active on this diet, you must dedicate considerable time to meal preparation, have some experience preparing and meal planning, and have access to a range of foods that can be very costly.

Additionally, eating out can be difficult due to prohibitions on common packaged foods, such as cooking oils. This can result in increased social alienation or tension.

Additional Pegan Diet Rules

Limit starchy vegetables such as potatoes or winter squash to 1/2 cup a day and go for low-sugar fruits like berries and kiwi. Beans should be used in moderation (less than 1 cup per day.)

Whole grains that do not contain gluten (teff, black rice, quinoa, and amaranth) can be consumed in moderation (1/2 cup per meal).

As an occasional treat, sugar in the form of maple syrup or honey can be consumed.

Occasional grass-fed, organic cow's milk dairy products such as ghee or kefir, provided they may not induce pain, may be consumed; sheep's milk and goat's milk products may also be consumed.

Foods should be processed minimally to remain as true to their natural state as possible.

Although alcohol is not specifically stated, it is usually prohibited on the Paleo diet.

"What I like about the Pegan diet is that it's another 'clean food' approach," says Carolyn Williams, PhD, RD, nutritionist for Cooking Light. "An focus is placed on whole grains, minimally refined foods, and natural fruit, as opposed to foods with added sugars or fat that might be less nutritious. Furthermore, I appreciate the focus on fruits and vegetables," she adds. "It would be lower in salt than the traditional American diet, and I like the fact that it is a bit more inclusive than Paleo."

Menu Example

Although the pegan diet is centered on fruits, it also incorporates sustainably raised meats, fish, nuts, and seeds. Certain legumes and gluten-free grains may be used in moderation.

A Sample Menu For One Week:

For Monday

Breakfast: Vegetable omelets with an olive oil-dressed green salad

Lunch: Salad with kale, chickpeas, almonds, and avocado.

Dinner: Wild salmon burgers with roasted carrots, steamed broccoli, and lemon vinaigrette.

For Tuesday

Breakfast: Sweet potato "toast" with diced avocado, pumpkin seeds, and lemon vinaigrette

Lunch: Bento box lunch of hard-boiled eggs, sliced turkey, raw veggie sticks, fermented pickles, and blackberries.

Dinner: Stir-fry vegetables with cashews, carrots, bell pepper, tomato, and black beans for dinner.

For Wednesday

Breakfast: Green smoothie with apple, spinach, almond butter, and hemp seeds for breakfast

Lunch: Vegetable stir-fry with leftovers

Dinner: Kabobs of shrimp and vegetables grilled on the grill, served with black rice pilaf

For Thursday

Breakfast: Pudding made with coconut and chia seeds, walnuts, and new blueberries

Salad with mixed greens, avocado, cucumber, grilled chicken, and cider vinaigrette for lunch

Salad with roasted beets, pumpkin seeds, Brussels sprouts, and sliced almonds for dinner

For Friday

Breakfast: Fried eggs, kimchi, and braised greens for breakfast.

Lunch: Lentil and potato stew with sliced cantaloupe for lunch.

Dinner: Salad with radishes, jicama, guacamole, and strips of grass-fed beef for dinner.

For Saturday

Breakfast: Overnight oats with cashew milk, chia seeds, walnuts, and berries for breakfast.

Lunch: Remaining lentil-vegetable stew.

Dinner: Roast pork loin with steamed vegetables, greens, and quinoa for dinner.

For Sunday

Breakfast: Veggie omelets with a plain green salad for breakfast.

Lunch: Salad rolls in the Thai theme, with cashew cream sauce and orange slices.

Dinner: Pork loin and vegetables that were left over.

10 Breakfast Recipes For The Pegan Diet

01. Smoothie With Strawberry, Banana, And Coconut Milkman

This smoothie has a delicious strawberry and cream taste. It's so creamy because of the coconut milk. Additionally, strawberries impart a traditional taste and a soft pink hue. The sugar in this coconut milk smoothie comes from a frozen ripe banana, but there are no extra sweeteners.

Quick tip: ice super ripe bananas to keep them on hand for smoothies. Often peel the bananas until freezing, so they can be frozen whole or sliced into chunks. Bananas that have been frozen are simple to slice or split into chunks when desired.

Of course, if you want a reduced carb version of this strawberry smoothie, you can omit the banana and sweeten to taste with stevia, monk fruit, or another low carb sweetener. In this scenario, I'd use frozen strawberries and a few ice cubes to hold the smoothie cold—-and coconut cream (scooped from the top of a can of chilled coconut milk) to add extra creaminess.

To achieve the extra-thick consistency, use full-fat coconut milk. Consider purchasing coconut milk in a BPA-free can or carton that has no contaminants. The list of ingredients should consist solely of coconut and water. It is safer to avoid refrigerated coconut milk, since it often contains gums or other refined food chemicals.

The addition of vanilla extract imparts an ice cream-like flavour to this strawberry banana smoothie recipe, which reminds me of a strawberry milkshake. I use organic vanilla paste, but you might also use vanilla powder or scrape the seeds from a vanilla bean.

02. Baked Eggs and Zoodles with Avocado on a Ketogenic Diet

With unlimited amounts of meat and cheese, the keto diet is very short, er, savoury. However, there are moments when you want something that would not leave you feeling just as weighted down. Enter ketogenic fried eggs and avocado zoodles. They're high in fat and protein and the ideal way to spice up breakfast or dinner.

Instructions:

1. Preheat oven to 350 degrees Fahrenheit. Grease a baking sheet lightly with nonstick oil.

2. Toss the zucchini noodles and olive oil in a big bowl to mix. Season with sea salt and freshly ground pepper. Divide the mixture into four equal parts, move to the prepared baking sheet, and form each part into a nest.

3. Gently crack an egg into each nest's base. Bake for 9 to 11 minutes, or until the eggs are ready. Salt and pepper to taste; garnish with red pepper flakes and basil. Accompany of avocado slices.

03. Vegan Vegetable Frittata

Vegan Frittata is an excellent way to use leftover vegetables and create a simple, affordable vegan meal that is suitable for breakfast, lunch, or even dinner!

Frittata is a traditional Italian dish made with eggs and whatever vegetables are available. In this vegan edition, we'll use an incredibly tasty tofu-based 'egg' mixture and an abundance of vegetables to create an utterly delectable vegan frittata!

Ingredients Needed

Tofu and spices are pureed to create a 'egg' mixture and combined with sautéed vegetables in this recipe. The mixture is then baked until golden on the outside and soft on the inside, making the perfect vegetarian vegan frittata.

All you'll need is listed below, along with suggestions for ingredient substitutions:

- Potatoes – every colour is appropriate, including white, red, gold, and russet (with or without the skin).
- Any colour onion would suffice.
- Bell pepper – use bell peppers of your preferred flavour.
- Cauliflower

- Substitute a couple of halved cherry tomatoes for the yellow squash.
- Garlic
- Silken tofu organic – solid or soft (silken pref.). Any tofus has a chalky flavour when pureed; you'll have to experiment to find one that tastes well to you. Generally, silken tofu does not taste chalky. There is no need to click the tofu.
- Unsweetened non-dairy milk – substitute your preferred plant milk.
- Cornstarch (preferably organic) – arrowroot or tapioca flour can be substituted.
- Yeast that is nutritional
- Mustard – dijon or whole grain mustard (sub with mustard powder)
- Tarragon – thyme or basil can be substituted (or any combo)
- Powdered garlic
- Turmeric
- Flakes of red pepper
- Season with salt and pepper.

Preparation Of Vegan Frittata

01. Preheat the oven to 375 degrees Fahrenheit.
02. To begin, make the tofu egg mixture by combining the tofu, nutritional yeast, dijon, cornstarch, garlic powder, herbs, red pepper flakes, and salt and pepper in the bowl of a food processor or blender and processing until smooth, scraping down the sides as necessary.
03. Then, on the stovetop, prepare the vegetables.
04. Until prepared, combine the sauce mixture with the cooked vegetables.
05. Finally, fill a 9-inch springform pan halfway with the vegan vegetable frittata mixture (or any 9 x 11 shallow dish will do).
06. Bake for about 40–45 minutes. The frittata pictured above was cooked for the entire 45 minutes.
07. And presto, you've got yourself a delectable vegan frittata to feed to family and friends!

04. Eggs with Asparagus and Tomatoes

Raise your hand if you're an egg lover. Now, if you despise sweeping, lift the other. To that end, allow me to introduce you to your new favorite recipe. This sheet-pan egg dish is practically the ultimate breakfast or dinner dish.

How to Prepare:

1. Preheat oven to 400 degrees Fahrenheit. Using nonstick cooking oil, grease a baking dish.
2. Arrange the asparagus and cherry tomatoes on the baking sheet in an even layer. Season with thyme and salt and pepper to taste. Drizzle the olive oil over the vegetables.
3. Roast for 10 to 12 minutes, or until the asparagus is almost tender and the tomatoes are wrinkled.
4. Season each egg with salt and pepper on top of the asparagus.
5. Return to the oven and bake for a further 7 to 8 minutes, or until the egg whites are fixed but the yolks are still jiggly.
6. Divide the asparagus, onions, and eggs into four plates to serve.

05. Vegan Paleo Pancakes

Vegan Paleo Pancakes are tender on the inside and finely fluffy on the outside. A delectable pancake that is suitable for anyone who live an egg- and grain-free lifestyle. For further delectability, drizzle with Roasted Strawberry Vanilla Bean Sauce.

Ingredients you will need:

- 1 cup almond flour
- 3/4 cup tapioca flour
- 1 tablespoon baking soda.
- 1/4 teaspoon sea salt.
- 2/3 cup almond milk, unsweetened

- 2 tbsp vinegar made from apple cider
- 1 tablespoon maple syrup
- 1 tablespoon melted coconut oil
- 1 teaspoon vanilla extract (pure).

Directions

01. In a mixer, combine all of the ingredients. Blend for a few seconds, then pause, scrape the edges, and continue blending for a few seconds longer. You can also make the batter in a bowl; but, as mentioned previously, blending helps to make these egg-free pancakes fluffier.

02. If necessary, add additional liquid or flour in tiny amounts (1/2 Tbsp. at a time) until the batter has the consistency of pancake batter.

03. Pour batter into a greased skillet over medium/medium high pressure, around a meagre 1/4 cup batter per pancake.

04. Flip pancakes as they begin to bubble or the spatula quickly falls under the pancake. Continue cooking until both sides are golden brown.

05. Allow pancakes to slowly cool before serving.

Toppings such as Roasted Strawberry Vanilla Bean Sauce and almond butter can be added.

06. Breakfast Skillet of Sweet Potatoes

A delectable breakfast that is ideal for weekend mornings. This Sweet Potato Breakfast Skillet is loaded with spinach, bacon, and eggs, which makes it the ideal one-pan dinner. This skillet is ideal for Whole30 breakfasts and is delicious for every dinner.

How To Prepare Sweet Potatoe Breakfast Skillet

Step 1: In a 10-12 inch cast iron skillet, apply the avocado oil (check to ensure the skillet fits in the steam oven first!), followed by the sweet potato, onions, and spices. Cook the sweet potato mixture for about 15 minutes on the stovetop over medium heat, or until the onions and sweet potatoes are softened.

Step 2: Apply the kale and bacon to the skillet. Combine the kale and sweet potatoes, then sprinkle the bacon on top to crisp and prevent the kale from frying. Bake the skillet for 10 minutes.

Step 3: Remove the skillet from the oven (careful of the very hot handle!) and make four divots in the mixture with a wooden spoon. Each divot should contain an egg. If you need to cook additional eggs, the skillet will possibly accommodate up to six. Reheat the skillet in the oven for 7-10 minutes, or until the eggs are ideal doneness.

Step 4: If necessary, garnish the skillet with sliced green onions. Otherwise, serve immediately.

This is an excellent choice for meal planning, so if you are just feeding yourself, enjoy one portion hot and pack the remaining portions for the next few days' meals. This keeps for 3-4 days in the refrigerator if kept in an airtight bag.

NOTES

Make this skillet your own by substituting different meats or vegetables. Consider substituting sliced broccoli or bell peppers for the kale. Substitute diced precooked pork for the bacon, or omit the meat entirely to make this a vegetarian skillet. Additionally, it's delectable with a slice of melted cheddar cheese on top!

Prior to beginning this meal, place your cast iron skillet in the oven to ensure that it slips easily and helps the door to shut. This recipe calls for a ten-inch cast iron skillet. If the handle is too long, a dutch oven may be used in place of a skillet.

07. Banana Muffins (Gluten Free)

A grain- and gluten-free banana muffin made simple in a blender or food processor! Bananas serve as the sole source of sweetness in these nutritious snacks. Serve simple or garnish with dark chocolate chips, almonds, or peas!

Ingredients:

- 380 grams bananas, or about three medium bananas, ripe
- 3 pastured eggs
- 1/4 cup melted pastured butter

- 1/3 cup SunButter No Added Sugar
- 1 teaspoon vanilla extract
- 1 teaspoon freshly squeezed lemon juice
- 1/3 cup coconut flour
- 1 teaspoon baking soda.
- 1/4 teaspoon sea salt
- dark chocolate chips on top, if desired
- Optional: pumpkin seeds on top

Directions:

01. Preheat oven to 350 degrees Fahrenheit. Fill a 12-muffin tray with parchment paper liners and set aside.

02. Combine the bananas, melted butter, eggs, SunButter, vanilla, and lemon juice in a food processor bowl or blender. Process until the mixture is smooth and creamy.

03. Process the coconut flour, baking powder, and sea salt before the dry ingredients are incorporated.

04. Fill the muffin tin halfway with the flour, evenly splitting it into 12 muffins.

05. You will decorate each muffin as you wish or make them simple.

06. Bake the muffins for 18-22 minutes, or until the muffin centres are fully cooked.

07. Allow about 5 minutes for the muffins to cool before attempting to remove them from the muffin pan. Leftover muffins can be stored in an airtight container in the refrigerator for up to 5 days or in an airtight container in the freezer for up to 3 months.

NOTES

Since coconut flour dries out easily, avoid overbaking these muffins. Slightly undercooked is preferable. Additionally, coconut flour performs best in baked goods after a day, which means the muffins will be extra fluffy on day two!

Why can you use lemon juice?

When sunflower seeds and sodium bicarbonate (baking soda) are combined, they react and turn green. A few drops of lemon juice tend to mitigate this reaction. If you use a certain nut or seed butter in this recipe, you should omit the lemon juice.

08. Breakfast Casserole of Sausage

This low carb breakfast casserole features spinach, all-natural ham, and caramelised onions. If you omit the cheese, this casserole is dairy-free. To make this keto-friendly, halve the onion quantity and omit the sun dried tomatoes. I like to cook this casserole the night before a special event, so that it's ready to bake in the morning. Additionally, it is an excellent choice for meal prep.

Ingredients:
- 1 bunch chopped lacinato kale
- 2 tsp avocado oil
- 1 finely sliced onion
- 1 tsp sea salt
- freshly ground black pepper to taste
- 1 Original No Sugar Pork Sausage Roll (ten ounces)
- 12 eggs
- 1/4 cup unsweetened almond milk (not vanilla)
- 1/4 cup full-fat coconut milk
- 1 cup sliced white cheddar cheese
- 1/4 cup thinly sliced sun-dried tomatoes

Directions:

01. Add kale to an 8×8 baking dish and set aside.

02. Then, over medium low heat, add the avocado oil and the thinly sliced onions to a skillet. Caramelize the onions over a low sun. This will take 15-20 minutes, so prepare the remaining ingredients while you wait for the onions to begin to brown. Season to taste with 1/2 teaspoon salt and freshly ground black pepper. Every couple of minutes, stir the onions to ensure even browning and avoid fire. Arrange the onions on top of the kale in the baking bowl.

03. Preheat the oven to 3500 F as the onions are browning. Low-temperature baking leaves this casserole extra soft.

04. Increase the heat to medium high and add No Sugar Pork Sausage Roll. When the sausage browns, use a spatula to break it up. Combine the browned bacon, spinach, and onions in the baking dish and scatter the ingredients thinly over the top of the dish with a spatula or fork.

05. Add eggs, almond and coconut milks (or dairy substitute), the remaining 1/2 teaspoon salt, and pepper to taste to a big mixing cup. Whisk in half of the cheese, if using.

06. In the baking bowl, pour the egg mixture over the vegetables and sausage. Sun-dried tomatoes and extra cheese can be sprinkled on top.

07. Bake the casserole, covered with plastic, for 30 minutes. Remove the foil and bake a further 20-25 minutes, or until the centre is set.

08. Serve immediately. Allow to cool slightly before storing leftovers in the refrigerator for up to 4 days.

Notes

To prepare this casserole ahead of time. Prepare it to the point of covering it in foil and storing it in the refrigerator overnight. In the morning, place it in a preheated oven and bake according to the directions. Additionally, the casserole can be cooked ahead of time and reheated for 20-25 minutes at 350 degree Fahrenheit.

09. Recipe for Sweet Corn Zucchini Pie

A refreshing summer dish or brunch extension! This summer-inspired vegetable torte cries summer. Serve alongside a light summer lunch or brunch! This summer-inspired vegetable torte cries summer. Serve with a side salad or fruit for a nutritious breakfast.

Ingredients:

- 4 medium zucchini, very thinly sliced
- 1 tsp olive oil
- 1 minced onion
- 3 ears sweet corn cut from the cob
- 1 teaspoon sea salt
- freshly ground black pepper to taste
- 3 pounded eggs
- 1 cup parmesan cheese

Directions:

01. Cut zucchini and summer squash quite thinly using a mandolin slicer or by hand.
02. 1 teaspoon sea salt and freshly ground black pepper, to taste, season pounded eggs.
03. In a frying pan over medium heat, heat olive oil and sauté onion for approximately 7 minutes, or until it starts to brown. Sauté sweet corn, salt, and pepper for an additional 2-3 minutes.
04. Preheat oven to 350°F. Line an 8-inch springform pan with parchment paper. This prevents the egg from seeping out of the pan's rim. If you don't have anything to line the plate, place it on a baking tray to trap any egg that escapes during the cooking process.
05. Cover the bottom of the springform pan with two coats of zucchini. Arrange 1/3 of the corn mixture and 1/3 of the cheese on top of the layer. Drizzle approximately 1/3 of the egg over the substrate to aid in its adhesion. Continue until there are four layers of zucchini and three layers of rice, butter, and egg.

06. Bake for 26 minutes on Bake/Reheat in the Sharp Superheated Steam Countertop Oven at 400 degree Fahrenheit.
07. Preheat oven to 400 degree Fahrenheit and bake for 40 minutes, or until the top is crisp and the eggs are thoroughly cooked.
08. Allow 20-30 minutes for setting before slicing.

10. Breakfast Bowls of Chocolate Chia Pudding

These breakfast bowls are not only delectable, but also very nutritious! Chia seeds are immersed in a mixture of coconut milk, water, and pureed dates until they reach a smooth pudding-like consistency. This dessert is delicious on its own or with fresh fruit and nuts on top.

Ingredients:
- 1 1/4 – 1 3/4 cup distilled water
- 1 3/4 cup canned coconut milk, full fat
- 4 ounces dates, soaked and drained
- 6 tbsp raw cocoa powder
- 2 tsp vanilla
- 3/4 tbsp. chia seeds.

Suggestions for Toppings
- fresh fruit
- nuts
- coconut (unsweetened)
- nut butter
- unsweetened diced dark chocolate

Directions:
01. To soften pitted dates, soak them in hot water. Drain well and set aside after soaking for 1-2 minutes.

02. Add water (start with 1 1/4 cup), coconut milk, cocoa powder, dates, and vanilla extract to a blender. Process on high speed until the dates are fully smooth and a rich creamy chocolate mixture forms.

03. Pulse to incorporate the chia seeds. Avoid excessive blending. The aim is not to merge the seeds, but to incorporate them.

04. This can be made in a bowl and mixed, but since chia seeds gel easily and bind together, I find it easier to extract them in a blender.

05. Allow about 5 minutes for chia seeds to soak before pulsing again. Repeat one more with the finest texture.

06. Enable chia pudding to soak for at least 1 hour in a sealed jar. If the pudding is too moist, apply additional water to thin it out until it reaches the perfect consistency.

10 Pegan Diet Entree Recipes:

Find below the exclusive 10 Pegan Diet Entree Recipes.

01. Keto Casserole With Broccoli And Ham

This simple casserole is brimming with goodness! It takes about ten minutes to combine all of the ingredients in a casserole tin, and then bakes with a cheesy crust on top. It's the ideal low carb meal that the whole family will support.

Ingredients

- 3 whisked eggs
- 1/3 cup strong whipping cream *seek pastured or grass-fed dairy products.
- 1/2 cup grated parmesan cheese
- 1 teaspoon sea salt
- Freshly ground black pepper to taste
- 6 cup rice de cauliflower
- 2 bundles Smoked Canadian Bacon.
- 4 cup florets de broccoli
- 2 cups cheddar cheese

Directions:

01. Preheat oven to 425 degrees Fahrenheit.
02. Whisk together the eggs, strong whipping cream, parmesan cheese, salt, and pepper in a medium-sized mixing cup.
03. Add the cauliflower rice, ham, broccoli, and egg mixture to a 9-inch casserole tray. Combine the ingredients with a fork.
04. Sprinkle the melted cheddar cheese on top of the casserole.
05. Bake the casserole, covered with foil, for 35 minutes. Remove the cover from the casserole and continue baking for a further 10 minutes to brown the cheese on top.

NOTES :

This recipe fits for frozen or fresh cauliflower rice. Enable frozen meat to partially defrost before adding it to the casserole dish. This tutorial will show you how to make homemade cauliflower rice.

Tip: If the cauliflower rice releases a lot of water, remove the excess water after cutting the foil before continuing to cook the casserole uncovered for the final 10 minutes.

02. Chicken Scarpariello

This traditional American-Italian recipe mixes tender braised chicken breasts, sausage, peppers, and onions in a flavorful white wine sauce with fresh herbs. The browned chicken skin provides the base for this dish's flavours, which are enhanced by caramelized onions and fresh rosemary. Give enough time for the chicken skin to tan and the onions and peppers to fully melt as the white wine decreases.

Ingredients

- Baby Potatoes Roasted
- About 1 1/2 pounds cocktail potatoes
- 1 tbsp olive oil sea salt
- Freshly ground black pepper to taste
- Scarpariello Chicken
- 8 chicken thighs
- season with sea salt to taste
- freshly ground black pepper to taste
- 2 tbsp olive oil
- 3 fried and sliced sweet Italian sausages
- 1 yellow onion, sliced
- 1 red bell pepper, sliced
- 3 minced garlic cloves
- 1 quart of white wine

- 1/4 cup vinegar made from white wine
- 1 cup chicken broth.
- Peppadew peppers or sweet pickled peppers 1/2 cup
- 3 new rosemary sprigs.

Directions:

Baby Potatoes Roasted:

01. Preheat the Sharp Supersteam Wall Oven to 450 degree F for 25 minutes on the Bake Mode.
02. Arrange baby potatoes on a baking sheet. Drizzle olive oil over the potatoes, after that season with salt and pepper. Coat the potatoes evenly with your mouth.
03. When cooking the braised chicken dish, bake the potatoes.

Chicken Scarpariello:

01. Season chicken thighs liberally with sea salt and pepper.
02. Preheat a big dutch oven over a moderate heat source. Add the olive oil to the pot, followed by the chicken thighs skin side down. Allow 5-7 minutes for the chicken skin to tan. Chicken thighs should be removed from the pan and placed aside.
03. Brown the sausage in the hot pan for about 5 minutes. Remove and set aside the bacon.
04. Add the onions to the hot pan and reduce to a medium low heat. For about 5-7 minutes, stir the onions as they continue to soften. Season with salt and pepper the red bell peppers and garlic. Continue to soften for another 7-10 minutes, stirring often to avoid fire.
05. Reduce the product by half by adding the white wine and white wine vinegar.
06. In a large saucepan, combine the chicken broth, peppadew peppers, and sausage. Stir the sausage into the onion and pepper mixture to incorporate it.
07. Nestle the chicken in the vegetable-sausage mixture and garnish with rosemary sprigs.

08. Following the removal of the potatoes from the oven. Bake at 350 degree F for 30 minutes.

09. Arrange the Dutch oven on a tray in the Steam Oven's bottom shelf.

10. Serve the potatoes with a chicken leg and a spoonful of the pepper and onion mixture, drizzled with white wine sauce.

NOTES:

This recipe needs patience to prepare properly. Take your time! Before adding the white wine, ensure that the onions are fully softened, and allow the white wine and vinegar to boil and reduce slightly before proceeding with the sauce. These steps aid in the concentration of flavours, resulting in a rich and aromatic broth.

Numerous variants: This braised chicken recipe can be made for any kind of chicken. Chicken breasts or drumsticks can be substituted for the chicken thighs. Increase the baking time to 40 minutes if the chicken breasts are high.

03. Thai Style Baked Pork Tenderloin

Thai flavours will enhance the taste of your pork tenderloin. Serve with a plain cucumber salad and rice for a restaurant-quality dinner.

Ingredients

- 1/4 cup coconut aminos or a suitable substitute 2 tbsp soy sauce + 2 tbsp water
- 3 tbsp rice wine vinegar de vinaigrette de rice
- 3 tsp lime juice
- 2 tsp sesame seed
- 2 teaspoons coconut sugar.
- 2 tbsp. grated fresh ginger
- 1 tablespoon minced garlic
- 1 tablespoon sriracha paleo
- 1 teaspoon sea salt
- 2 pound pork Tenderloin.

Directions:

01. Whisk together all of the ingredients except the pork in a tub.

02. Cover the pork tenderloin with the marinade in an airtight tub. Marinate for 2 hours to midnight, rotating the tenderloin once or twice during the marinating process to ensure even marinating.

03. Preheat the Sharp SuperSteam+ Built-in Wall Oven to 485 degrees Fahrenheit using the SuperSteam Grill.

04. Preheat the oven to Broil while using a traditional oven.

05. Pork should be placed in a baking dish, and the stored marinade should be poured into a small saucepan.

06. Bake for 15 minutes, or until the internal temperature of the pork tenderloin exceeds 1450 F for a medium-cooked tenderloin. Other cooking temperatures are mentioned in the notes section below.

07. If using a traditional oven set to Broil, switch the tenderloin over halfway through the baking period and check the internal temperature at this point and at 3-4 minute intervals afterwards.

08. Reduce the marinade by half over medium low heat, stirring regularly.

09. To separate the blocks of ginger and garlic from the marinade, strain it through a wire sieve.

10. Allow 10 minutes for the meat to rest before slicing. Drizzle the reduced sauce over the top or serve the sauce on the side.

NOTES

The tenderloin's internal temperature will begin to climb for a few minutes after it is removed from the oven. I normally remove my pork tenderloin from the oven three to four degrees below the temperatures mentioned below.

135 degree – Moderately Rare

145 degree - Medium

160 degree – Well Done

04. Vietnamese Lettuce Wraps with Beef

These Vietnamese Beef Lettuce Wraps are a delectable and enjoyable lunch or dinner recipe that are bursting with flavour. A short beef marinade, grilling the steak, and preparing a flavoured nutty sauce are all simple and convenient meal prep options.

Ingredients:

Marinated Steak

- Grass-fed sirloin steaks, 12 oz.
- 3 tablespoons coconut amino
- 1 teaspoon sea salt
- 3 tsp lime juice
- 3 teaspoons finely minced lemongrass
- 2 garlic cloves, finely minced
- 1 finely minced shallot

'Peanut' Sauce (Vietnamese)

- 1/4 cup SunButter Unsweetened
- ¼ cup coconut milk
- 1/4 cup coconut aminos
- 2 tbsp rice wine vinegar
- 2 tsp lime juice
- 1 tsp sesame oil
- 1 to 3 tbsp paleo sriracha

Wraps of Beef in Lettuce

- 1 head butter lettuce
- 1 cup julienned carrots
- 1 cup thinly sliced purple cabbage
- 1 cup basil, fresh
- 1/2 cup mint, fresh
- 2 tbsp sesame seeds.

Directions:

Steak Marinade

1. In an airtight container, combine the steaks and marinade ingredients and toss to coat the steaks. Marinate the item for at least one hour and up to 24 hours. If you don't have time to prepare this a day in advance, you should thinly slice the steak and marinate it for one hour.

Sauce of Sunflower "Peanuts"

01. In a blender, combine all of the sauce ingredients and heat until very creamy. Refrigerate or set aside until ready to use. The remaining sauce keeps well in the refrigerator for up to a week and makes an excellent vegetable dip or salad dressing.
02. Wraps of Beef in Lettuce
03. On a stand, arrange lettuce leaves and then garnish with herbs and vegetables.
04. If necessary, barbecue the steak on an outdoor grill to desired doneness. If cooking outside is not necessary, fire a cast iron pan over high heat and sear both sides of the steak in avocado oil. Reduce heat to low and continue cooking until desired doneness is achieved.
    01. Allow the steak to rest, covered with foil, for 10 minutes before slicing. Thinly slice the steak and split among the lettuce wraps. If required, sprinkle with sesame seeds.

NOTES

Any sort of lettuce would work, but I like the butter lettuce's softness and pliability. It can be challenging to locate. Romaine and leaf lettuce, as well as big cabbage leaves, are both excellent choices.

If you're having difficulty locating grass-fed beef, consider ButcherBox. It's an excellent way to guarantee that you're receiving the highest-quality meats (delivered directly to your house!), without having to look for them. I appreciate hearing that they are doing experiments on my behalf and that the meat I am serving my family is hormone- and antibiotic-free.

Combine the vegetables in these wraps! Additionally, I like adding thinly sliced red peppers and red onion.

05. Wraps Of Thai Chicken Lettuce (Whole30)

These Thai Chicken Lettuce Wraps are a healthy alternative to take-out. The chicken is ginger-infused, and the rich, nutty sauce completes the dish. And so nutritious as well! Carbohydrate-restricted, Paleo, and Whole30 compatible.

Ingredients:

Lettuce Wraps

- 1 romaine lettuce head
- 1 cup shredded red cabbage
- 1 cut mango
- 1/2 cup roasted sunflower seeds, or almonds or cashews.
- To garnish red chilies, use cilantro and Thai basil. conceivable

Chicken with Spicy Ginger

- 1 tsp sesame oil
- 1 pound ground chicken can be substituted for 1 pound ground turkey.
- 1/4 cup grated fresh ginger
- 1/4 cup minced Thai shallots
- 2 tbsp coconut amino acids (can sub Tamari or soy sauce)
- 1/2 tablespoon chilli sauce(or more, to taste)
- 1/4 teaspoon sea salt.
- Almond Sauce (Thai)
- 1/4 cup unsweetened almond or sunflower seed butter
- ¼ cup coconut milk (full fat)
- 1 tbsp rice wine vinegar.
- 1 and 1/2 tbsp coconut aminos
- 1/2 teaspoon freshly squeezed lime juice.

- 1/2 tsp chili sauce
- 1 tsp sesame seed oil
- pinch of seasoning salt to taste

Directions:
1. In a skillet over medium-high pressure, heat the sesame oil and add the ginger and shallots. Cook for 7-10 minutes, or until the vegetables are very tender and fragrant.
2. Brown the field chicken. To taste, season with sea salt, coconut aminos, and chili sauce.
3. To make the Sun Butter sauce, combine all of the ingredients in a blender and process until smooth. You can also achieve this with a cup and a simple brush, but it will take longer and the mixture will be cleaner if you use a blender. Keep the SunButter sauce refrigerated until ready to use.
4. To assemble the wraps, layer cabbage, mango, and chicken in the middle, followed by toasted seeds and herbs on top.
5. Serve with spicy Thai SunButter sauce drizzled on top or on the foot.

NOTES

Meal prep these: Thai lettuce wraps are an excellent choice for meal prep. If the chicken and sauce are prepared, you can prepare the remaining vegetables, such as chopping bell peppers, mangos, and cabbage, or toasting sunflower and sesame seeds for garnish.

When you're about to eat, gather your ingredients and stuff some crisp lettuce leaves!

If you've prepared these in advance, the sauce can thicken until chilled. Allow the sauce to come to room temperature before whisking it again until it is light and fluffy.

Make these nut-free by omitting the nuts: This are nut-free if the Thai lettuce wrap dipping sauce is made with sunflower seed butter and the wraps are topped with toasted sunflower seeds.

Reduce the Carbs: Omit the mango to make these Whole30 Lettuce Wraps low carb or keto.

06. Salad with Spinach and Bacon Dressing.

This Spinach Salad with Bacon Dressing is a festive and beautiful salad for your holiday table. It features roasted delicata squash, pomegranate, and pecans. It's easy to prepare ahead of time and assemble for your special dinner.

Ingredients

- 8 cups baby spinach
- 2 roasted delicata squash
- 1 cup arils de pomegranate 1 pomegranate, big
- 1/2 cup toasted pecans
- hot bacon dressing

Directions:

1. Delicata squash can be roasted.
2. Prepare your Hot Bacon Dressing according to the directions on the package. This dish can be prepared in advance and reheated for your special dinner. It's easy to make — cook the bacon, fry the shallots in the bacon fat, and then throw the crumbled bacon, sweetener, and vinegar back in. It's a truly exclusive salad dressing!
3. Layer lettuce, delicata squash, pomegranate, and pecans on a platter or in a salad bowl to assemble the salad.
4. Toss the salad with the spicy bacon dressing just before eating. If your holiday party includes vegetarians, serve the dressing on the side and have a substitute, such as this Poppy seed Honey Mustard, or even only balsamic vinegar and olive oil.

Note:

Veganize it: Except for the sauce, this salad is vegan as published. Rather than a spicy bacon salad dressing, try my Poppy seed Honey Mustard Dressing or a plain combination of lemon juice, balsamic vinegar, and olive oil.

Make a Meal of It: Rather than serve this as a side dish, elevate it to a special dinner by including additional protein. This is delicious served with fried chicken, hard-boiled eggs, or roasted chickpeas.

If delicata squash is unavailable, substitute blocks of butternut squash or cut and roasted acorn squash. Acorn squash, like delicata squash, can be roasted in the same manner as delicata squash.

07. Roasted Beef Tenderloin

After you've tried this decadent beef tenderloin roast, you could just replace your holiday turkey with it! A flavorful garlic and rosemary butter imparts incredible taste to this tender steak! Serve with roasted broccoli, mashed potatoes, or a plain green salad to highlight the tenderloin. We suggest beginning the roasting process the day before. A day before, a sea salt and pepper rub guarantees the finest crust around your roast.

Ingredients

- 3 pound roast beef tenderloin
- 1 teaspoon sea salt
- Freshly ground black pepper to taste
- 4 tbsp salted butter
- 4 minced garlic cloves
- 1 tablespoon chopped rosemary
- 1 teaspoon mustard dijon

Directions:

1. Tenderloin roast should be tied with kitchen twine. This is accomplished by evenly spreading individual pieces of twine around the roast every 2-3 inches.
2. Season with salt and pepper the roast. Refrigerate it exposed overnight.
3. Preheat the Sharp SuperSteam+ Built-In Wall Oven to Steam/Roast mode for 15 minutes at 450 degrees Fahrenheit.
4. Combine melted butter, rosemary, garlic, and dijon mustard in a shallow dish. Combine the ingredients thoroughly.
5. Arrange the roast in a single layer on the baking sheet. Coat the roast with the butter mixture.

6. Roast the beef for 15 minutes on one hand, then turn it over and pick "more time" to add another 10 minutes. After ten minutes, check the internal temperature of the roast with a meat thermometer, referring to the map below for optimal doneness. Cook the roast for a further 5-10 minutes at a time before it reaches the desired temperature.

7. Allow 10 minutes for the meat to rest before slicing it.

NOTES:

Guide to Internal Temperatures:

Exceptional – 115°F – 120°F

Moderate Exceptional – 120°F – 125°F

Medium - 130°F – 135°F

Serve with roasted broccoli. Coat 2 lbs. broccoli in 1 tablespoon olive oil and season with salt and pepper to taste. While the roast is resting, place the broccoli tray in the oven and set the timer to "additional time" for 7 minutes.

Preheat oven to broil. Place the roast on the middle rack of the oven and cook for 10 minutes, or until the roast's top begins to brown. Turn the roast over and cook for about the same amount of time on the other side.

Reduce the oven temperature to bake at 450° F and bake until preferred doneness is achieved using an oven thermometer.

08. Sausage Spaghetti Squash Boats

This is a delectable way to eat pasta night without the carbohydrates! Spaghetti squash boats baked in the oven make a tasty low carb dinner. These are topped with melty mozzarella cheese and a sausage and veggie sauce. The recipe begins with a baked squash, so prepare accordingly!

Ingredients:

- 1 baked spaghetti squash
- 1 tsp avocado oil
- 1/2 cup chopped onion

- 1/2 cup chopped green bell pepper
- 1/2 cup sliced black olives
- 1 package sliced Golden Brown Chicken Sausage.
- 1 and a half cups marinara sauce
- 1 cup mozzarella cheese

Directions:

1. Preheat oven to 450 degrees Fahrenheit. Prepare a halved baked spaghetti squash for stuffing.
2. Add avocado oil, onions, and bell peppers to a skillet. Saute for approximately 10 minutes over medium low heat, or until they are translucent.
3. Add olives, sliced sausage, and marinara sauce to the skillet. Bring to a low heat and then turn off the heat.
4. Arrange the baked spaghetti squash cut side up in a baking dish. Loosen the strands from each squash half with a fork.
5. Fill half of the sauce and half of the cheese into each squash half.
6. Bake the stuffed squash for approximately 10 minutes, or until the cheese has melted and begun to brown.

09. Soup With Chicken, Zoodles, And Sweet Potatoes (Thai Red Curry)

This Thai-inspired soup is brimming with chicken, sweet potatoes, and zoodles that are fun to eat. It's a fantastic Whole30-approved soup that's packed with satiating fats, protein, and plenty of vegetables. Contains no added sugar or preservatives!

Ingredients:
- 1 tbsp avocado oil (or substitute olive oil)
- 3 minced garlic cloves
- 3 tbsp. grated ginger
- 1/2 tsp turmeric

- 2 cups broth (vegetable or chicken)
- 1/4 cup SunButter Unsweetened
- 2 tbsp Thai red curry paste *makes a very spicy soup – adjust the heat accordingly
- 1 pound cubed or thinly sliced chicken breasts
- 1 large peeled and cubed sweet potato
- 1 14-ounce can full-fat coconut milk
- 1 red bell pepper, thinly sliced
- 1 cup thinly sliced red onion
- 3 tbsp coconut aminos
- 2 tbsp. lime juice
- 1 zucchini, approximately 6 cup zoodles (1 very large zucchini)

Directions

1. In a large soup pot or dutch oven, heat the avocado oil, garlic, ginger, and turmeric over medium heat. Saute the aromatics for approximately 5 minutes, or until they are softened.
2. Add a splash of vegetable broth to the pot, along with the red curry paste and SunButter. After whisking to form a creamy paste, add the chicken, sweet potatoes, and remaining vegetable broth. Allow to simmer for approximately 15 minutes, or until the chicken is cooked and the sweet potatoes are softened.
3. Bring to a simmer the red peppers, onions, and coconut milk. Coconut aminos and lime juice are used to season the soup. Season the broth with sea salt to taste, if necessary. Allow approximately 5 minutes for the vegetables to soften.
4. While the soup is cooking, create zoodles using a spiralizer. If you do not have a spiralizer, you can either use a vegetable peeler to create long strands of zucchini or simply chop the zucchini.
5. To serve, spoon zoodles into bowls and top with hot soup. If desired, garnish with cilantro and green onions.

10. Creamy Tuscan Garlic Chicken

This is a dairy-free, Whole30-approved version of an Olive Garden classic recipe. This version is rich and creamy, with sun dried tomatoes, a sprinkling of spices, and a smidgeon of lemon.

Ingredients

- 4 chicken breasts about 2 pounds
- 1 tablespoon olive oil
- salt and pepper

Creamy Garlic Sauce

- 1/2 tablespoon olive oil
- 1 onion (diced)
- 4 cloves garlic (thinly sliced)
- 1/2 cup sun dried tomatoes chopped
- 1 teaspoon basil (dried)
- 1/2 teaspoon oregano (dried)
- 1/2 teaspoon rosemary (dried)
- 1/2 cup chicken broth
- 3/4 cup almond milk
- 1/2 cup coconut milk
- 1 teaspoon lemon juice
- salt and pepper

Instructions:

01. In a pan, melt the olive oil over medium-high heat.
02. Season the chicken with salt and pepper.
03. Brown the chicken on both sides, then cover and cook until finished, about 15 minutes.
04. Remove the chicken from the pan.
05. Reduce the heat to mild and add the olive oil.
06. Sauté for 5 minutes with the garlic and onions.
07. Season the sun dried tomatoes with salt, pepper, and Italian herbs in a pan.

08. When the garlic and onions are fragrant, add the chicken broth and cook until almost all of the liquid has evaporated.
09. Bring the almond milk and coconut milk to a medium simmer. Season with salt and pepper to taste after adding the lemon juice.

10 PEGAN Diet Recipe For Dinner:

You will find below the 10 exclusive Pegan Diet Recipe for dinner.

01. Salad Of Pan-Seared Salmon, Kale, And Apple

The kale salad is the star of this dish. It's crunchy, sweet, and tart all at the same time!

Ingredients:

- 4 Salmon fillets, 5 oz., center-cut (about 1" thick)
- 3 tbsp freshly squeezed lemon juice
- 3 tablespoons olive oil
- Kosher salt
- 1 bunch kale, ribs removed and leaves sliced very thinly (about 6 cups)
- ¼ cup dates
- 1 apple (Honeycrisp)
- 1/4 cup pecorino cheese, finely grated
- 3 tbsp slivered almonds, toasted
- Black pepper, freshly ground
- 4 dinner rolls made entirely of whole wheat

Directions:

01. Ten minutes prior to cooking, bring the salmon to room temperature.
02. In a large mixing bowl, whisk together the lemon juice, 2 tablespoons olive oil, and 1/4 teaspoon salt. Toss in the kale and set aside for 10 minutes.
03. While the kale is standing, shave the dates and apple into matchsticks. Toss the kale with the dates, apples, cheese, and almonds. Season with salt and pepper to taste, toss well, and set aside.
04. Season the salmon generously with 1/2 teaspoon salt and freshly ground pepper. In a large nonstick skillet over medium-low heat, heat the remaining 1 tablespoon oil.

Increase the heat to a medium-high setting. In the pan, place the salmon skin-side up. Cook about 4 minutes until one side is appears golden brown. Turn the fish over with a spatula and continue cooking for approximately 3 minutes longer, or until it feels firm to the touch.

05. Evenly distribute the salmon, salad, and rolls among four plates.

02. Slow Cooker Spicy Beef Curry Stew

This hearty, spicy beef stew is only for the brave. While I prefer to make it in the slow cooker, it can also be made on the stovetop. Excellent with mashed potatoes or rice.

Checklist of Ingredients:

- 1 tsp olive oil
- 1 pound beef stew meat
- Salt & pepper
- 2 minced garlic cloves
- 1 teaspoon freshly grated ginger
- 1 diced jalapeno pepper, fresh
- 1 tsp curry powder
- 1 (14.5 oz) can diced tomatoes
- 1 sliced and quartered onion
- 1 cup beef broth.

Instructions:

Step 1

In a skillet over medium heat, heat the olive oil and brown the beef on all sides. Season with salt and pepper and remove from skillet, reserving juices. In a skillet, cook and stir the garlic, ginger, and jalapeno for 2 minutes, or until tender. Season with curry powder. Combine the diced tomatoes and juice in a medium bowl.

Step 2

Layer the onion and browned beef in the bottom of a slow cooker. Combine the skillet mixture and beef broth in the slow cooker.

Step 3

Cover and cook on Low for 6 to 8 hours.

03. Wraps Of Tempeh Lettuce With Peanut Sauce (Vegan)

Cook the tempeh in a nonstick pan to avoid a translucent filmy layer forming on the bottom of the pan. If you are using a nonstick pan, the filmy layer will be more difficult to remove.

Ingredients:

- 8 oz. tempeh block
- 1 cup broth made from vegetables
- 1 teaspoon soy sauce (use tamari if gluten free)
- 1 tsp maple sugar
- 1/4 teaspoon coriander, ground
- 1/8 teaspoon powdered garlic
- 8 butter lettuce leaves
- 1 medium peeled and julienned carrot
- 1: 1 1/4 cup red cabbage, thinly sliced
- 1 medium red bell pepper, sliced
- peanut sauce

Directions

01. Transfer the tempeh cubes to a food processor and cut them into 1/2 inch cubes. Blend the tempeh for approximately 5 seconds, or until very small pieces of tempeh remain. When you open the lid of your food processor, you will smell the fermented soy beans, which is perfectly normal.

02. Combine the vegetable broth, soy sauce, maple syrup, garlic powder, and coriander powder in a bowl.

03. Over medium heat, heat a nonstick skillet or sauté pan. Combine the tempeh and broth mixture in a medium bowl. Cook, stirring occasionally, for approximately 8 to 9 minutes, or until the liquids have completely absorbed into the tempeh. While the tempeh may appear to be ready to remove from the heat in five minutes, resist the urge. When you tap the tempeh with the back of a spatula and hear a sound akin to walking through puddles in the rain, this indicates that the tempeh is not yet ready. You're probably off by a few minutes. Remove the pan from the heat once the liquid has been absorbed.

04. Arrange the lettuce wraps in a single layer. Carrots, cabbage, red bell pepper, and some tempeh should be stuffed into the lettuce leaves. Drizzle peanut sauce over the filling and, if desired, garnish with scallion slices and red pepper flakes. Serve right away.

NOTES:

Substitutions:

You may substitute sugar for the maple syrup. If you are not vegan, you may substitute honey or agave for the honey or agave. Additionally, you can substitute romaine lettuce or any other lettuce variety that you have on hand for the butter lettuce.

04. Salad With The Ultimate Chicken Tacos

Ingredients

- 4 cups chicken shredded (1 rotisserie chicken)
- 1 tablespoon ghee
- 1 teaspoon paprika
- 1/4 teaspoon cumin
- 1/2 teaspoon chilli powder chipotle (chili powder is fine too)
- 1/2 teaspoon garlic powder
- 1/4 teaspoon oregano, dried
- 1 tbsp paste de tomato
- 1/4 cup chicken broth
- 1 teaspoon salt, kosher
- 1/4 teaspoon freshly ground black pepper

- 1 head romaine lettuce, cut into salad-size pieces
- 1 medium watermelon radish (or 4 regular radishes), thinly sliced and diced
- Pico de gallo
- 2 avocados, thinly sliced
- 1 lime, sliced
- Avocado Ranch Dressing Tessemaes

Directions

01. Melt ghee in a skillet over medium heat. Add paprike, cumin, chipotle chili powder, garlic, and oregano once the ghee has melted. For approximately 1-2 minutes, toast herbs and spices. After the garlic is fragrant, add the tomato paste and stir to combine. Whisking constantly, slowly add chicken broth to the paste + spice mixture until well combined and transformed into a thick sauce.
02. Toss the chicken in the skillet to coat evenly with the sauce and cook until the chicken is just heated through. Season again with salt and pepper and toss.
03. Divide the romaine, radish, pico de gallo, and avocado among four salad bowls. Serve with chicken and a lime slice on top. Drizzle with Avocado Ranch dressing from Tessemaes.
04. Take pleasure!

05. Sweet Potato Pizza Crust

Three-ingredient sweet potato pizza crust – only sweet potatoes, rolled oats, and an egg are required! SUPER EASY, HANDS-ON, HEALTHY PIZZA CRUNCHY!

Ingredients

- 3 x 1 medium peeled sweet potato
- 2/3 cup oats, rolled
- a single egg
- 1/2 tsp salt
- a smattering of garlic powder
- 1 tsp olive oil

Directions

01. Preheat the oven to 400 degrees Fahrenheit. Pulse the sweet potato and oats until very fine. Pulse again to combine the egg, garlic powder, and salt. The mixture should have the consistency of a soft dough or a thick batter.

02. Transfer to a baking sheet lined with parchment paper or a round pizza pan. Shape with your hands into crusts – you can either make two smaller crusts (for a more crispy edge surface area) or one larger crust. Crusts should mea21sure between 1/4 and 1/2 inch thick.

03. Bake for 25-30 minutes, or until the top feels dry. Remove from oven, cool slightly, and invert back onto the pan, dry side down. Gently peel away the top layer of parchment and brush with olive oil. Continue baking for an additional 5-10 minutes to achieve a nice crispy top.

Add your preferred pizza toppings and return to the oven to melt the cheese! That is all.

Notes:

When you peel away the parchment paper, the crust will adhere to it. Simply proceed gently and cautiously – it should work perfectly, and even if a few tiny pieces of crust fall off with the parchment, the crust will remain intact. If this is a serious problem, return it to the oven for a few minutes with the parchment paper ON TOP to dry it out. This would make it more manageable. If you're concerned about the hand-hold ability, I'd let the crust cool and dry slightly before baking. High-moisture toppings such as tomato sauce and mozzarella cheese may wreak havoc on this crust's hand-hold ability and can necessitate fork action. We discovered that the BBQ Chicken pizza toppings (BBQ sauce, chicken, cheese, red onion, and cilantro) were the most likely to yield a hand-hold able crust right after baking.

06. Salad Of Thai Mangoes And Avocados With Grilled Sweet Potatoes

Ingredients:

- 250g 1 medium sweet potato, peeled and quarter-inch thickly sliced
- 1 tablespoon melted coconut oil
- 1 cup mango (180g)
- 1 big avocado, cubed, 120g
- 2/3 cup sliced cucumber
- 1/4 cup thinly sliced and finely packed fresh mint
- 1/4 cup Cilantro, fresh, diced and packed
- Sea Salt

To make the sauce:

- 4 tsp. Lime Juice
- 2 tsp Fish Sauce, Paleo-friendly

Instructions

01. Preheat your barbecue to high heat. Toss the sweet potato slices in the coconut oil and grill for 3-4 minutes per hand, or until pleasant grill marks form. Once cold enough to treat, slice them into tiny cubes and add them into a big dish.

02. Add in the pineapple, banana, cucumber, mint and cilantro and whisk until mixed.

03. Mix the lime juice and fish sauce in a small bowl and spill over the salad. Toss to mix.

04. DEVOUR!

07. Roasted Vegetable & Lentil Salad With Coriander Yoghurt Dressing

Chili roasted carrots, light peppery puy lentils and the most wonderful fragrant coriander yoghurt dressing. This easy but flexible salad is perfect if you choose to make lunch boxes or cook to impress! Vegan, GF, paleo & healthy.

Ingredients

- 2 tiny sweet potatoes peeled & sliced into 1 inch cubes
- 100 g (1/2 pack) chestnut mushrooms quartered
- 10 cherry / plum tomatoes
- 1 yellow pepper (1/2 inch strips)
- 1/2 head broccoli sliced into florets
- 1/2 tbsp olive oil
- 1 tsp chili flakes
- Sea salt & freshly ground black pepper
- 100 g (1/2 cup) dry puy lentils/lentil's vertes

For The Dressing

- 15 g (1/2 bunch) new coriander
- 2 tbsp raw yoghurt
- 1 clove garlic peeled
- Juice of 1/2 a lemon
- Pinch of sea salt
- 60 g (1 bag) (1 bag) wild rocket
- 15 g (1/2 bunch) coriander leaves only
- 1 red chili thinly sliced.

Directions

01. Preheat the oven to 170°c fan/190°c/375°f.

02. Line a baking tray with parchment paper and spread over the sweet potato. Roast for 10 minutes.

03. Remove the tray from the oven and apply the onions, onions, pepper and broccoli to the sweet potato. Drizzle over the oil, chili flakes and a generous pinch of salt and pepper before offering it a blend. Return to the oven for another 30-35 minutes before the vegetables are tender and cooked through.

04. Meanwhile put the lentils in a medium sauce pan and cover with cold water. Bring the pan to boil before reducing the heat and simmering gently for 18-20 minutes before tender. Drain and put aside.

05. To make the dressing add the coriander, yoghurt, garlic, lemon juice and salt into a blender / food processor. Blend until smooth. Taste and change the seasoning if desired.

06. To assemble, combine the rocket, lentils and 2/3rds of the roasted vegetables together in a big dish. Transfer onto a serving platter and finish with the remaining roasted veg, coriander and chili slices. Liberally drizzle over the dressing and eat!

NOTES

This salad can be eaten hot or cold! To serve cold only cause all the components to cool fully before assembling and storing in the fridge. Add the dressing right before serving.

This salad is perfect for lunch boxes as it lasts very good for an up to 4 days in the fridge. I like to make a double batch of this roasted vegetable and lentil salad at the beginning of the week to hold for a fast and nutritious lunch.

You can mix up the veggies in this salad to whatever you have at home / what is in season. I love this with courgette and aubergine too - just mind the cooking times can vary!!

To make this salad vegan just substitute the yoghurt for a gluten free option such as soya yoghurt in the dressing.

08. Mexican Toasted Corn Quinoa Salad

This Mexican toasted corn quinoa salad is a simple nutritious weeknight dinner great for anyone in a hurry. Made in under 25 minutes, filled with flavour and filled with protein this scrumptious salad won't leave you hungry. Perfect as a primary or side dish. Vegan, Gluten-Free & Paleo.

Ingredients

- 100 g (2/3 cup) quinoa rinsed
- 1/4 vegetable stock cube
- 1 tsp rapeseed / olive oil
- 200 gm tin of sweet corn drained
- 100 gm (large handful) cherry / plum tomatoes (quartered)
- 1 big handful coriander finely chopped
- 4 spring onions thinly sliced
- Juice and zest of 1 lime
- 1/2 tsp chili flakes
- 1 ripe avocado peeled and sliced
- Generous pinch sea salt.
- Freshly ground black pepper

Directions

01. Fill a medium saucepan with water and add the stock cube and quinoa, whisk and bring to the boil. Reduce the heat and simmer for 15-18 minutes until the quinoa is tender. Drain and put aside.

02. Meanwhile, heat the oil in a frying pan over a medium heat. Add the corn and pinch of salt and pepper and fried for 5 minutes or so until the sweet corn is golden brown and slightly crisp. Remove from the sun.

03. In a big bowl add the cooked quinoa, 3/4 of the sweet corn, 3/4 of the avocado and all the remaining ingredients. Stir well to mix.

04. To eat, split the salad into two plates before garnishing with the remaining sweet corn and avocado.

NOTES

This salad is perfect hot or cold! To serve cold cause both the quinoa and sweetcorn to fully cool. Then mix with the remaining ingredients and refrigerate.

If you plan to pre-make this Mexican toasted corn quinoa salad, skip the avocado (so it doesn't brown), store the pre-made salad in an airtight jar in the fridge for up to 3 days and substitute the avocado just before eating.

And sure that your tinned sweet corn hasn't got any extra sugar or salt. The ingredients can read 'sweet corn, water' only. It is best to apply the salt yourself!

09. Sweet Potatoes With Lemony Kale And White Beans

Affordable, wholesome, and simple to cook, sweet potatoes topped with lemony kale and white beans makes a tasty meal every day of the week; ideal for meal prep.

Ingredients

- 4 medium/large sweet potatoes
- 1 Tbsp olive oil, optional
- 1 shallot or other onion, diced
- 1 to 2 cloves garlic, minced
- 1 tsp lemon zest cost included in the lemon mentioned below
- ½ to 1 tsp sea salt, to taste
- 1 bunch kale, thick stems cut, chopped (can replace collards, baby kale, chard, spinach, etc) (can substitute collards, baby kale, chard, spinach, etc)
- 1 (15 oz) may Cannellini beans (about 2 cups cooked beans) (about 2 cups cooked beans) For herbal,
- ½ to 1 tsp crushed red pepper flakes (optional)
- juice from half a lemon.
- toasted tamari pumpkin seeds

Instructions

01. Preheat oven to 350 degrees. Wash and dry sweet potatoes. Prick the tops a couple times with a spear. Place on a baking sheet and bake until tender, about 45 to 60 minutes depending on height.

02. Preheat a sauté pan over medium heat. Add the grease, if using. Add the shallot and simmer for about 2 minutes, stirring regularly. Add the garlic, lemon zest, and salt, and simmer for 1 minute. Add the kale, beans, and red pepper flakes and continue to cook, stirring regularly, 2 to 3 minutes, or until the kale is wilted and deep green. Add the lemon juice. Taste for seasoning and change when required. Remove from sun.

03. Allow sweet potatoes to cool slightly. Top each one with the kale and bean mixture. Or if this is meal prep, cause it to cool. Store the potatoes and bean mixture individually in the refrigerator for up to 4 days.

10. Baked Salmon With Black Rice

Baked Salmon with Black Rice can be baked in the oven and ready in less than thirty minutes. It's made of good for you heart balanced omega-3 fatty acids. {gluten free}

Ingredients

- 3 4 oz salmon fillets
- 1 cup black rice
- 2 cups water
- ½ cup sugar snap peas
- 3 tbsp dried cranberries
- 1 tsp garlic powder
- 1/2 teaspoon salt
- 1/4 teaspoon pepper
- 1 tbsp zest de orange

Directions

01. To make rice, combine 1 cup black rice and 2 cups water in a rice cooker. Alternatively, on the stovetop, bring 2 cups water to a boil and apply the rice and salt. Cook on low heat for about 30-35 minutes, or until rice is soft.

02. Preheat the oven to 400 degrees Fahrenheit. Garlic, lime, and pepper the salmon. Cook for about 15-20 minutes on a baking dish.

03. When rice is cooked, add snap peas, cranberries, salt, and pepper immediately. Arrange salmon on top and garnish with orange zest. Season with salt and pepper to taste. Garnish with sprigs of rosemary. (additional)

The Gist

The pegan diet is a combination of paleo and vegan values — but it does provide for some meat intake.

It places a premium on whole foods, especially vegetables, while generally avoiding gluten, dairy, the majority of grains, and legumes.

It is nutrient dense and may help support good fitness, but can be too limiting for other individuals.

You should experiment with this diet to see how the body reacts. If you are either paleo or vegan and want to change your diet, the pegan diet could be more manageable.

Made in the USA
Las Vegas, NV
05 December 2023

81964231R00031